Choosing and Caring for Garden Shrubs

PENNY PINCHA

GW01465753

Contents

Introduction

The value of shrubs is immense, particularly for the hobby gardener with only limited leisure time and cash to spare. Compared with most other groups of garden plants, shrubs are the most likely to give a lifetime's service in return for the minimum amount of maintenance and, where space is at a premium, they make ideal substitutes for the larger-growing trees.

Semi-mature or established specimens are usually expensive items to purchase, but on the whole the cost of a young shrub works out at little more than one would expect to pay for a decent house plant and therefore compares favourably when its life expectancy is taken into account. Efficient modern propagation techniques have helped to keep shrub prices down to economical levels and container production methods make it feasible to plant at almost any time of the year, provided ground and weather conditions are suitable.

The major factor that has contributed most to the rising popularity of shrubs is probably the all-year effect that many types provide. The seasonal herbaceous perennials, like delphiniums, chrysanthemums and bulbs, etc, give a display for only relatively short periods in the year, leaving bare areas of ground as they die back and enter their resting period. Winter is particularly lacking in colour, but a few well-chosen shrubs can provide interest in the form of flowers, brilliant fruits or foliage—indeed, the bare branches of certain shrubs are desirable for the general outline they form, or because of striking bark colour.

Apart from the obvious decorative qualities, shrubs can also fulfil many practical functions in the garden. They are ideal in the role of living screens or hedges along a boundary, and may be used to partition off various areas of the garden to good effect.

Climbing shrubs are particularly adept at transforming large bleak areas of walls and fences, while many unsightly tree stumps have been given a new lease of life when covered with a vigorous climber such as wisteria or clematis.

Where restricted space permits only the odd shrub or two to be planted in the border, the shade and protection they afford can be beneficial to many lower-growing herbaceous or annual plants nearby, particularly those that dislike exposed conditions. Where, however, you have a vast area of bare soil, but massed plantings of seasonal flowers is perhaps impracticable, then the ground-hugging, mat-like evergreen shrubs can make ideal ground cover.

It is this versatility that makes shrubs indispensable, for they can be used in all situations and soils. It is quite feasible to devote an entire garden to shrubs, large or small, without losing anything in the way of colour, interest or overall effect.

Hints on Choosing

Before actually going off to the local garden centre to buy some shrubs, consider the sort of soil and situations you have to offer them. Knowing just how much room there is to spare is important, for overplanting can be very wasteful as well as detrimental to the plants.

Although the majority of shrubs will thrive in any good garden soil that has been well prepared before planting, certain groups have special soil requirements. Rhododendrons and camellias are just two of the ericaceous shrubs that heartily dislike soils containing lime (alkaline), and are only really happy when grown in ground which is acid and rich in humus materials like leaf mould or peat. There are various ways in which the gardener can alter the physical condition (structure) of soils, but attempting to change the chemical composition can be a long, costly and usually frustrating business, so it pays to choose those shrubs that are known to grow well locally on your particular soil type.

The situations available for planting shrubs should also be considered before buying. Although you may have your heart set on some particularly fine form of the sun-loving potentilla, it's no use condemning it to live in the dense shade cast by tall trees or buildings; far better to opt for one of the shade-lovers like camellia or hydrangea, both of which revel in gloomy conditions. Remember that no amount of feeding can persuade a plant to change its 'nature', and given unsuitable quarters it may produce flowers and fruit only reluctantly, if at all. Ultimately it may present such a wretched sight that the only course left will be to grub it out and replant with something more accommodating.

Although a young shrub may look just the thing to fill up the odd gap in a border, remember that it will grow up eventually. Some naturally dwarf shrubby conifers are very slow growing, so perhaps they are the ideal choice for giving a rock garden some 'high-level' greenery without ever getting out of hand in a lifetime; but others have a prodigious growth rate and could swamp all the surrounding plants in just a few years from planting. Checking on the ultimate height and spread of a shrub is therefore good sense.

Where an entire new shrub border is required, you can plant the scheme so that the 'backbone' of permanent varieties of varying shapes and growth habits is spaced out sufficiently to allow for maximum spread over the years. But to relieve the initial bareness between these, interplant with a temporary assortment of quick-growing 'filler' plants. These can comprise shrubs like buddleias or roses, both renowned for instant effect, or a selection of herbaceous perennials, bedders and bulbs—all can gradually be removed as the main shrub planting requires room for expansion.

Examples of some different types of shrubs

5

Hints on Buying

First-time gardeners are often confused by the terms used by nurserymen to describe the condition of the roots on saleable shrubs, for depending on the time of year and plant type they may be variously offered as bare-rooted, balled, containerized or ex-pots. The condition of the roots at purchasing time is extremely important, as it could well mean the difference between the plant becoming established rapidly and failing to grow at all.

Bare-rooted shrubs are sold completely devoid of soil and are therefore offered only during the dormant season. Accept only deciduous shrubs in this condition, and ensure that most of the foliage has dropped. A bare-rooted plant retaining leaves is always in

A pre-packed shrub

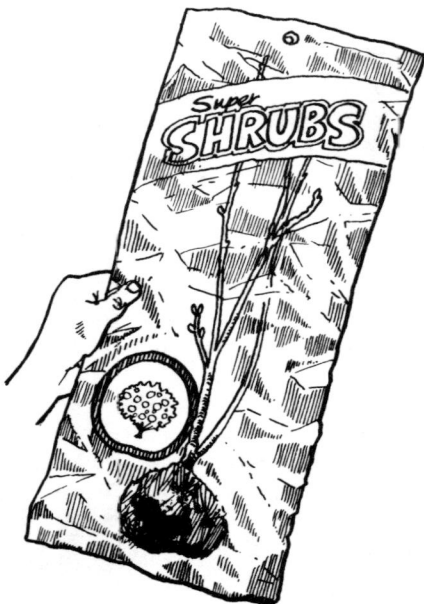

danger of dehydrating and eventually shrivelling up, a condition that can occur if it is stored for any length of time in warm and dry shops or selling areas. So be particular about what you accept in the way of rose bushes and other shrubs offered pre-packed in polythene display packs.

Bare-rooted stock plunged or heeled in outside beds are generally safer buys than those kept in a shop or under cover, for they are subjected to lower temperatures and are thus less inclined to shoot prematurely. Such shoots are usually very weak and drawn, prove extremely susceptible to frost damage, and, when produced in the depths of winter, do nothing but sap the stored-up energy of the shrub.

Balled shrubs are those that have been lifted from the ground complete with a substantial amount of soil adhering to the root system. This root ball is carefully wrapped in polythene or hessian to prevent it from drying out and falling apart, and thus is better suited to getting established in its new quarters. Evergreen and deciduous shrubs are offered in this condition, but again both are best planted during the dormant season. In the case of evergreens, however, the planting period can be slightly extended into the beginning of the growing season in spring and at the latter part of summer, just before the trees become dormant.

When offered balled-up roots, make sure that the soil ball is moist and not breaking up. Also make sure that sufficient roots are present to support the top growth initially—the larger the shrub, the bigger the root ball should be also. Avoid shrubs bearing a root ball that is riddled with perennial weeds, particularly those like couch and ground elder that can soon cause widespread havoc in the garden.

Containerized shrubs are now extremely popular for they can be planted literally all year round, provided the soil is adequately moist and in a workable condition. Unlike the bare-rooted or balled shrubs, these can be safely left unplanted for long periods without much attention if planting is delayed, and, as the root system is completely intact they usually take less time to become established.

Select container shrubs that are well established in the compost—those where the roots have reached the sides of the container—but avoid those that have a pot-bound root system which curls tightly round the inside of the container and is firmly rooted into the standing ground or beds. Pot-bound shrubs will take longer to get established in your garden and could also be an indication that the stock is old and starved of nourishment.

The term 'ex-pots' is self-explanatory: the plants have been grown in containers and tipped out to facilitate easier packing and to keep plant and postage charges down to a minimum. The nurseryman will usually ensure the plants arrive in good condition by wrapping the small root balls in paper or polythene film.

When you make a personal selection of shrubs at the nursery or garden centre, make sure that the plants you buy are perfectly healthy. Refuse weak-growing specimens with pallid leaves and any that show signs of disease or starvation, for these will probably fade away after a time and could well introduce trouble to your garden. Look for signs of pest damage on the plants; although pests can be dealt with, their presence could indicate that the stock has not been properly looked after in the nursery, and other 'hidden' faults could well exist.

Semi-mature shrubs should bear a well-balanced framework of branches and be in the prime of health, with clean foliage if you buy in the growing season. Avoid conifers with patches of 'burnt' foliage, for this is difficult to rectify, and refuse those shrubs in either a growing or dormant state which show extensive areas of die-back on the shoots.

Finally, one note of warning if you order shrubs from a nurseryman's list: don't delay ordering the plants. It's usually a case of first come, first served, so if you have selected a new or very popular shrub, the longer you delay, the greater your chances of receiving a 'sold out' notice.

Avoid buying pot-bound shrubs

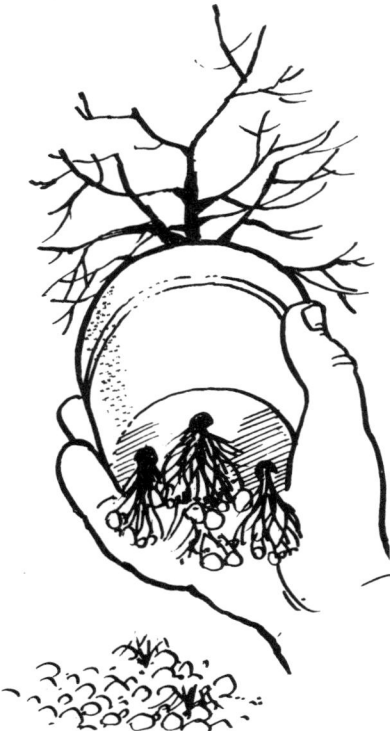

General Site Preparation

Whenever possible, all the planting sites should be prepared well in advance of buying the shrubs. This is particularly important if you intend to plant during autumn, for the plants will begin to arrive just as heavy rain or frost can be expected, both of which will bring work to an abrupt halt.

Most essential is the early completion of all the cleaning and heavy digging work. When you want to complete the planting in autumn, start work during September, earlier if conifers are your choice. Sometimes our unpredictable weather will make working impossible even in early autumn, but try to finish preparatory cultivations by November. If this is not possible it may be more practical to delay planting until the spring.

If the ground is wet enough to make the soil cling to your shoes, or it's frozen solid, leave it until conditions improve. You will only compact wet soil down into a badly drained morass if you walk on it, and turning over frozen soil may only slow down thawing, thus delaying planting work even further.

If the planting site is fairly extensive, it pays to prepare the whole area thoroughly rather than the individual planting stations. Ensure that all weeds are removed before or during digging. An application of weedkiller containing paraquat should deal effectively with most annual broad-leaved weeds, but deep-rooted types, like dandelions, docks and thistles, should be removed by hand. Weeds with creeping underground rootstocks may take considerable labour to clear, but if the top

Remove deep-rooted weeds by hand

growth is treated with a brushwood killer some time before you start digging, they should be weakened quite drastically.

Individual planting holes or trenches are also best prepared as early as possible, particularly if bad weather conditions threaten to delay work before plants can be purchased. If you take out the holes when the soil is in an ideal condition, the mound of infill soil can either be covered with a piece of polythene sheeting or taken under cover where it will not become saturated by heavy rain. When frost threatens to freeze the infill soil, some sacking placed over the mound should ward off the worst effects.

Where a specimen shrub is wanted in a lawn, mark the area to be cut out using two sticks at either end of a piece of string for circular beds, or a stout board and square edge for rectangles. Carefully remove the turf with a spade and use this for general lawn repairs, or throw it, grass side down, into the bottom of the planting hole.

Method of marking out a circle

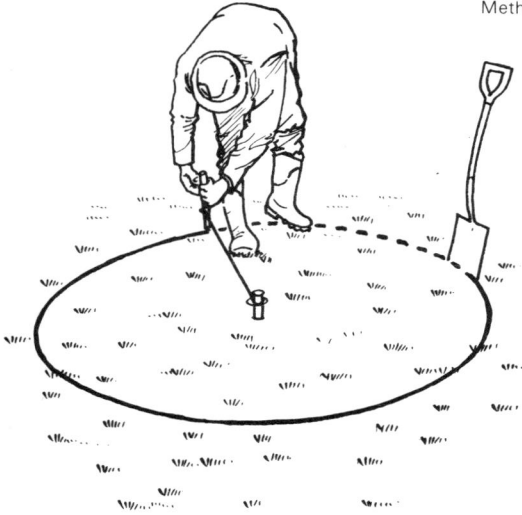

Turf should be placed grass side downwards in the planting hole

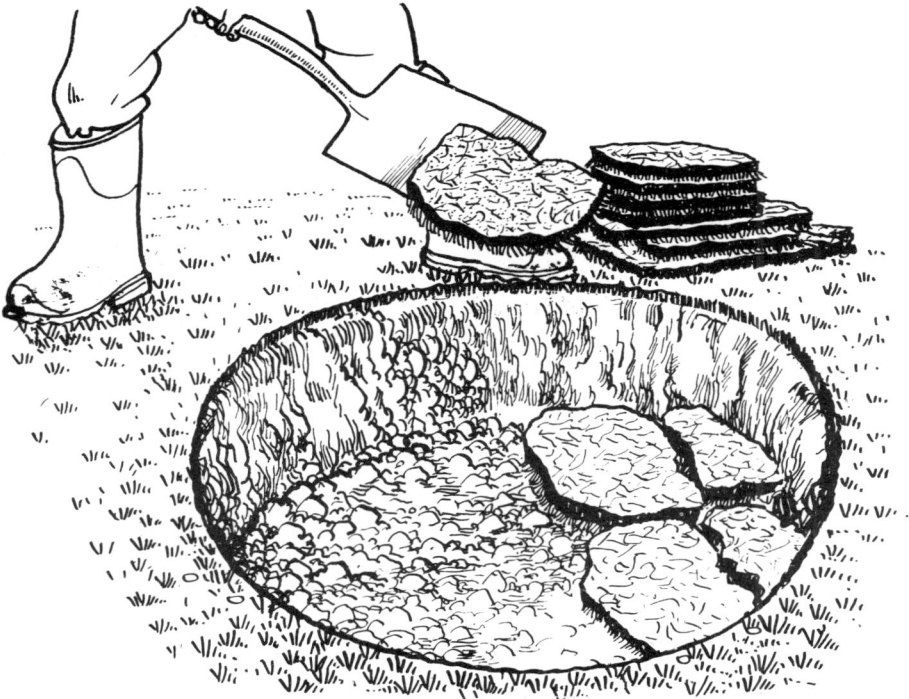

Digging and Soil Improvement

Light, well-drained soils may need to be dug only one spade depth (spit) deep, but heavy soils like clay are best double-dug in the following fashion.

Start at one end of the border and excavate a trench across the plot about 45.5cm (18in) wide and a spit deep, depositing the soil at the opposite end of the border. Fork over the base of the trench, then begin to turn soil from the bed on to this to form the second trench. Continue in this fashion up the plot until you come to the end, then fill in the final trench with soil from the first one.

Deep digging is important, for this will help to improve drainage and soil aeration, both essential for healthy root development, but it will not permanently improve soil structure. Fine soils will return eventually to their original sticky and compacted state, so to make the improvement permanent, you will need to add plenty of humus-forming materials like peat, garden compost and rotted manure as you dig the site.

Add compost and manure when digging to improve the soil

Humus helps to bind the small particles together into crumbs, thus allowing moisture and air to move freely in the soil. Sharp grit or sand will also prove beneficial on very heavy ground, but as large quantities may be needed to treat the whole area, its use can be confined to the individual planting holes.

Bulky materials like peat, etc, should be thrown into the trenches and well turned into the bottom spit when you double dig an area. Where single digging is carried out, lay the material at the base of each row of freshly turned clods and cover them with the next row.

Humus-forming materials are also ideal for improving the water and plant-food-retention qualities of light, severely draining soils like sand and gravel. Where ground is excessively drained, rain quickly runs down into the subsoil, taking much plant food with it, and so reducing the fertility. In hot summer periods, these soils tend to dry out very rapidly, a condition that will only aggravate the starvation problem.

The importance of improving the soil before planting cannot be overstressed, for most shrubs dislike being disturbed at the roots once established in their permanent quarters. And, as they are long-lived, there is little chance of rectifying any preparation neglected at this crucial time. Any subsequent deep cultivations to make good the omissions may only serve to damage shrub root systems, checking growth and performance.

Where soil is very heavy, it is best to dig the site in autumn so that the large sticky clods are exposed to the elements over winter. Wind, rain and frost will all do a good job in breaking the clods down, so that the soil is in a workable condition in the following spring. Lighter soils are usually much easier to work and are in planting condition fairly quickly, but whatever type of soil you garden on it's a good idea to leave the area for a month or so at least, so that the ground has a chance to settle.

Try to keep off freshly dug ground as much as possible, otherwise you may only compact it and undo all your hard work. If the ground is left for any length of time, however, you may find some weeds re-appearing so some hoeing or weedkiller application may make it necessary to walk on the site. Once the job has been completed, retrace your footsteps and fork out all footmarks.

Treatment Before Planting

Plants often arrive from the nursery when planting cannot be done immediately, but you should take measures to prevent the roots becoming dry or frozen. This is particularly important for bare-rooted plants which have little protection, but the same goes for balled or container shrubs. If they appear dry on arrival, give them a good soaking in water for an hour or two.

If the plants are likely to be out of the ground for only a short period, it should be enough to place them under a wall or fence, out of the wind and sun, and cover the roots with moist sacking. In very cold weather, however, it is better to place bare-rooted and balled shrubs in a shed or garage where the roots are less likely to freeze.

This is also good advice when container shrubs are purchased in hard weather, as the soil is easily frozen and should not be planted as such; a blanket of sacking or straw wrapped round the container, however, will often keep frosts at bay when the shrubs have to be stood outside.

Where conditions delay planting for long periods, the solution is to heel your shrubs in a trench taken out in a protected spot in the garden. Make the trench about a spit deep, sloping one side so that the shrubs can be laid at an angle, then cover the roots with soil and lightly tread it down.

In early autumn and late spring, there is a possibility that the ground

Soak the roots in water

If shrubs cannot be planted immediately, set them in a trench and cover lightly with soil

Treading in

could dry out, so periodically soak the soil as the need arises to prevent the roots being damaged. The temptation to put off planting containerized shrubs is often fatal, especially during the summer months, so take great care to supply these with adequate water.

The addition of some liquid fertilizer is also recommended for those that have filled the compost with a mass of roots, so that vigorous growth is maintained until the time when the shrub is finally set out in the open.

Tips on Planting

When you come to plant shrubs in a border, it's a good idea to try moving them about on the site to get the best effect. Arrange them so that the taller varieties lie to the back of boundary borders, or, if an island bed is being planted up, choose the most suitable types to form one or more 'high spots' towards the centre.

It's essential to give the plants plenty of room to expand, although where low-growing shrubs are wanted to relieve bareness beneath standard trees, these can come within 30cm (12in) or so of their taller kin. Try to position evergreens where they will provide focal points of interest in the winter months and unless the whole bed is composed of evergreens, avoid grouping all these together.

Where winter bark colour is required, such shrubs are best placed in front of a conifer or other evergreen subject, which will provide an excellent foil for the branches and coloured twigs.

Before planting, check the roots for any signs of damage and prune affected areas back to sound, healthy tissue. Also remove any dead roots that could well encourage fungus disorders after planting. Large cuts should be painted with a wound dressing for the same reason. If bare-rooted shrubs appear a little dry, it's a good idea to soak them in a bucket of water for an hour or two before planting. Balled or containerized plants are best given a

Before planting move the shrubs around to find the best arrangement

Remove the plastic container

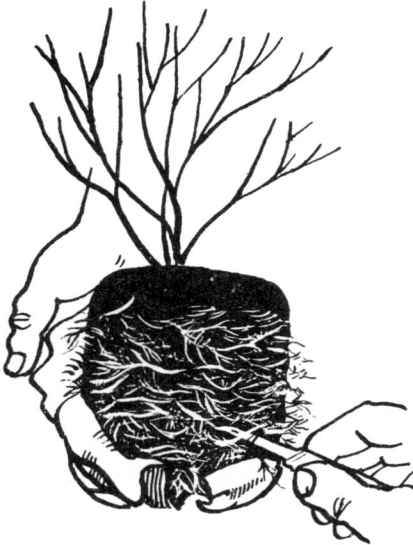

Trimming the roots

Gently tease out the roots

thorough watering beforehand.

Sacking or containers are best removed after the shrub has been placed in the hole, just in case the root ball crumbles. Where the soil is prone to drying out, it is often an advantage to leave the wrapping materials under the root ball, but where polythene is used, make a few slits with a knife to allow drainage, and tease out the roots. Sacking will rot away slowly in a year or two. Where shrubs are bought in metal containers, cutting them out may prove troublesome, but most garden centres supplying these will slit the container sides for you.

If there are any weeds in the root ball or container soil, make sure these are removed, especially the rampant deep-rooted ones like bellbind (convolvulus) and couch grass, or they will soon spread in their comfortable new quarters and smother everything in their path. Suckers growing up from grafted rootstocks, like roses, should also be cut off with a sharp knife, for, if allowed to grow, they could weaken the scion variety above and may eventually take over.

How to Plant

If your shrubs are to get established quickly, and remain stable in the soil, it's essential to plant them at the correct depth. Always make the planting holes large enough to take the roots comfortably; and, where overall site preparation is not practical, the wider the planting hole, the better the plant will grow.

Generally, you should be able to position the shrub so that the nursery soil mark on the stem is at ground level when the hole has been filled—in other words, it will be at the same level in your garden as it was in the nursery. The only exception to this rule is on very heavy, badly drained clays, when it is sometimes better to plant the shrub slightly higher than usual and make a mound of soil over the top of the root system. This method ensures better drainage and reduces the risk of waterlogging at a time when the roots are trying to get established.

Make the planting hole deep enough to take the roots plus a decent layer of good soil on which, ideally, they are set. Also make it wide enough to take the roots comfortably, without having to curl the ends up the sides of the hole. Never take the easy way out by cutting the roots down to fit a small

Fork over the base of the hole

16

hole—this practice will only have an adverse effect on the shrub and increase the risk of wind rocking the plants out of the ground in the first year of planting.

Where the soil from the hole has to be thrown on to the lawn, it's a good idea to lay down a sheet of polythene first, as this makes life a lot easier when you come to tidy up after planting is completed. It also makes mixing easier, when soil-improving materials and fertilizers are added to the infill soil.

The addition of peat, sharp sand or grit and some slow-acting fertilizer, such as bone meal, is beneficial where soils are poor. In fact, if it has not been possible to prepare the whole area thoroughly earlier, they are essential for good growth and health. On extremely poor soils a general fertilizer would prove helpful, but avoid any which release lime if you are planting ericaceous plants like heathers.

Once you've dug out the hole to sufficient depth, fork over the base well, mixing in as much well-rotted manure, peat or garden compost as you can spare. Provided the soil is not particularly 'sticky', you can now lightly tread the base down and add a generous layer of peat or mixed infill soil to bring the plant up to the correct level. A cane or board laid across the hole will help determine whether the plant is deep enough.

Improve the soil by adding peat and fertilizer

How to Plant

Any staking that is deemed necessary should be done before filling in, otherwise the roots could be damaged. Select a stout cane or stake of appropriate length and knock this down between the roots so that it runs parallel with the main stem a few inches away from the shrub. Provided a shrub carries a good root system little or no staking should be necessary, but firm supports will be needed by any with poor root balls and by tall standard shrubs like roses. Knock the stake down to the point just below where the branches break out from the main stem and secure with one or two plastic shrub ties or strong garden twine. Proprietary ties are recommended as they last for several years and are less likely to constrict stems.

Once the shrub is secured to the stake, start to fill in round the roots with the infill soil, working it in using either your hands or your heel. If some moist peat is thrown on to the roots first, this will help to prevent drying out in the initial growth period. But remember that it's essential not to leave air spaces, so firm the soil periodically as you fill the hole.

When the hole is filled to ground level, give a final firming down, then soak the area well if the soil is dry. If planting is done in late spring or summer the ground will quickly dry out, so an application of moist coarse peat or compost as a mulch will help to conserve soil moisture. Mulches are not recommended, however, during late autumn or winter, as they tend to hold frost, which does not encourage rapid root growth.

Finally, go over the whole area when planting has been completed and lightly fork out all footmarks.

Carefully position the roots

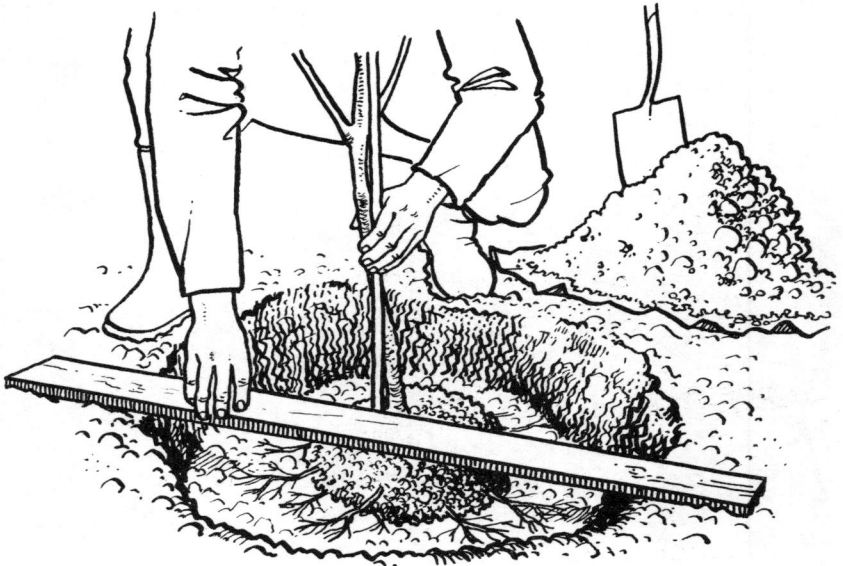

Work the soil in around the roots

Once planted, give the shrub plenty of water

To conserve moisture, add mulch to the soil

After-care

Drought can be a major problem for newly planted shrubs, especially during spring and summer when hot sun will dry out the ground rapidly. This problem can also occur during colder times of the year when frost 'freezes' ground moisture. The latter does not pose too much of a problem to deciduous shrubs that sink into dormancy in autumn, but some evergreens that put on some growth slowly in winter may be affected.

The way to reduce drought problems is either to maintain adequate moisture levels in the soil round the roots, or to reduce water loss through the leaves. Regular thorough soakings—a couple of good canfuls for small shrubs, or leaving a slow-running hose on larger specimens—will help during hot weather, but mulching the surface with rough peat or other water-retentive materials will go a long way to conserving soil moisture and

will help keep watering to a minimum.

Wind, especially cold drying wind during autumn and early spring, is a common cause of death with newly planted young shrubs. Evergreens are particularly vulnerable, so it's a good idea to give them some temporary protection, at least for the first year or so. Fairly small shrubs can be sheltered from wind by surrounding them with a windbreak formed of proprietary plastic netting secured to three or four stakes set in the ground at intervals around each shrub. Cheap polythene film can also be used in a similar way, but this does have a tendency to tear and get blown away after a time.

Where an extensive shrub planting has been made, say in a new border or where a hedge has been set out, screen netting can be stapled to stout posts lined up on the side facing into the prevailing wind. Rolls of hessian are also very useful in this context and less expensive.

A more recent idea to reduce moisture loss from evergreen shrubs is a plastic-type liquid spray called S 600;

Method of protecting one or more shrubs

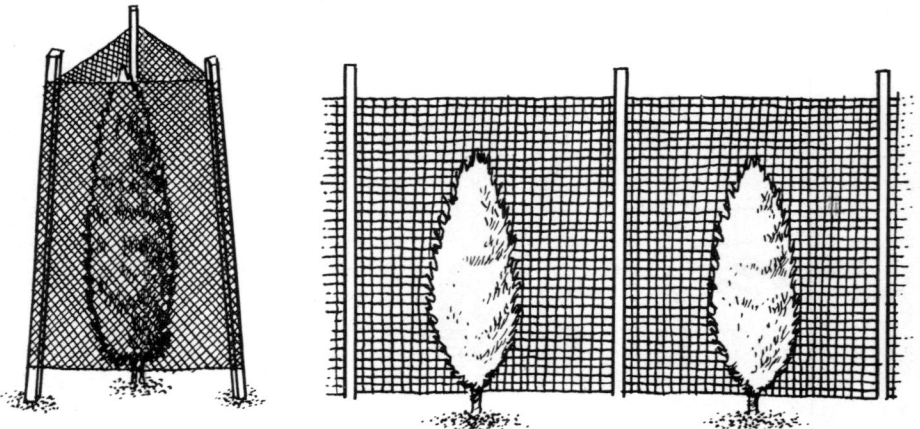

this is applied to the foliage and dries to form a protective film. Using this up-to-date method is certainly worth while for choice or fairly small shrubs, but could prove rather expensive where extensive planting is done.

In rural areas, shrubs may also need some protection from the ravages of hungry wild animals during the lean winter months. Rabbits and other small rodents are often forced to resort to eating bark in severe weather, so wrapping main stems with one of the proprietary spiral stem protectors is a preventive measure worth taking. Temporary winter cages of wire netting set over small choice shrubs will also deter rodent pests—they are also ideal if you live in an area frequented by wild deer, an animal that can clear quite high fences to get at any appetizing plants in the garden.

It's also a wise precaution to clear away all leaf litter or dead tall grass from the bases of shrubs. If this is left over the winter it will provide a snug home for mice who will take advantage of the convenient supply of bark if they should become 'snowed in'.

Weed growth must be discouraged at all times by hoeing, but where a mulch has been laid down few if any weeds are likely to be a problem under the shrubs themselves. If you do need to hoe or prick over the soil near the plants, however, don't go deep enough to disturb root growth, especially around surface rooters like rhododendrons and heathers. Once shrubs are established, a variety of long-acting herbicides may be applied to give weed control, but check label directions as a precaution against any possible limitations of use.

From time to time, check that supports are firm, but not tight enough to restrict expanding growth. This is es-

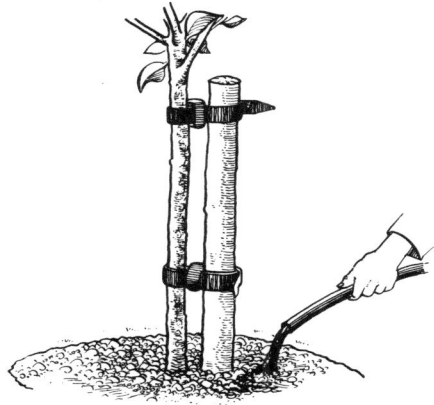
Method of tying a young shrub

pecially important if string or plastic-covered wire has been used, for these materials don't 'give' like plastic ties and shoots could well become constricted, causing a weak point that may well snap in high wind.

Loose ties are also a danger, for they will allow movement during windy weather and cause chaffing of the bark—always an entry point for disease. Insufficient support can also lead to tall shrubs being rocked about, the roots being loosened in the soil, which may cause the shrub to topple over.

If the planting site has been well prepared, little feeding should be necessary for a year or two, but if your soil happens to be on the poor side, an annual application of general balanced fertilizer scattered around the shrubs will help keep them vigorous. This can be gently worked into the surface of the soil with a hoe or, if the ground is dry, watered in.

Constant vigilance should be maintained against pest and disease attacks. These, and pruning methods, are dealt with under their appropriate headings in other parts of the book.

Pruning

Pruning is a job that causes some concern to many amateur gardeners, but if you take the trouble to find out the growth and flowering habits of your shrubs, and you prune at the right time of the year, then it's not as difficult as it may appear.

Pruning is necessary for a number of reasons, the foremost being to keep shrubs in shape. Wind, among other things, will break branches out from time to time and this will upset the general shape of a shrub, particularly if it has a prominent upright habit. If the terminal leading shoot is destroyed, often a bushy head will form which may not be typical of the variety; pruning will be necessary to encourage it to regain its natural form again.

Cutting off dead wood

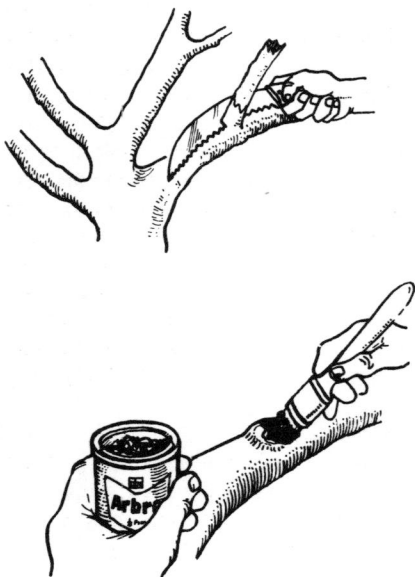

If dead or damaged branches are not pruned they may well become infected with disease, so prompt action should be taken to prevent this. Diseases will soon get a hold on the branches and within a short time you may well find widespread infection that is beyond control. If diseased wood is spotted, cut it out, even if it's not the recommended pruning time, taking the shoot or branch off at a point well into healthy tissue for safety.

Loss of the main terminal or leading shoot can ruin the appearance of a specimen shrub, so you should select a strong sideshoot to grow away to replace it. Cut the broken shoot off at a point just above the first strong sideshoot and encourage the latter to grow upright by tying it to a cane. If no suitable sideshoot is present, then cut the damaged leader out carefully to prevent disease, and from the flush of sideshoots that develop, choose the best for training up. If a tangled head of sideshoots results, it's a good idea to thin them out, removing the weakest to prevent overcrowding and congestion.

The degree of pruning a shrub will need is determined in part by its growth habit, but the encouragement of prolific flowering or foliage production may also be a major consideration. Shrubs like the hybrid tea or floribunda roses and the butterfly bush (buddleia) need severe annual pruning to maintain a compact well-flowered appearance. Left to themselves for a year or two they will develop tall, bare, woody stems, which give blooms at high level only.

Less severe cutting may be needed by shrubs such as the common flowering currant, *Ribes coccinea*, which, like its fruiting cousins, prefers to have only a proportion of the older unproductive

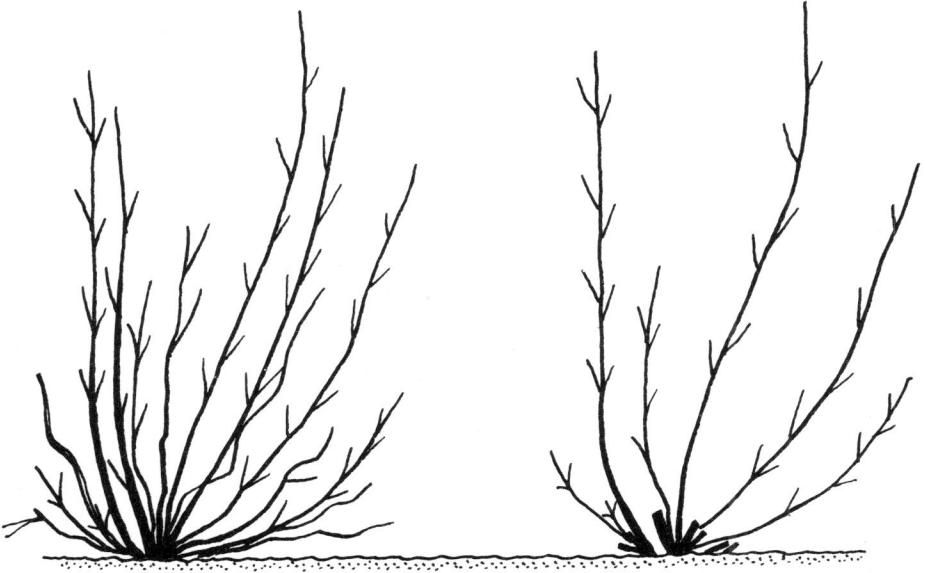

Prune older branches and weak shoots to encourage vigorous new growth

stems removed each year. In contrast, less vigorous subjects like rhododendrons may need only a minimum of pruning, if indeed any.

As a rough guide, use the vigour of a plant as a pointer to the severity of the pruning required, but take care that the operation is carried out at the appropriate time of the year to avoid cutting away wood bearing flower buds.

Those shrubs that produce their flowers on new wood—shoots produced in the current year—are normally pruned before flowering and fairly early in the season. Floribunda and hybrid tea roses, and the common buddleia, are typical examples, the common practice being to cut them back in late autumn or early spring. There is a danger, however, that when hard cutting back is done before frosts have ended, shoots encouraged to 'break' into early growth during a mild spell could be badly damaged.

This may result in a loss of flowering shoots, but one way round the problem is to prune only lightly in autumn. Then if the shoots breaking into growth at the ends of branches do get blasted by cold you can prune back yet again to encourage replacement growth from dormant buds lower down.

Forsythias, most flowering evergreens and rambling roses, all of which flower on wood made in the previous year, are best pruned after flowering. Forsythias often need fairly heavy pruning to encourage a flush of vigorous branches and should be pruned quite soon after the blooms have faded, but less rapid growers like currants (Ribes) can be left until the summer months or the autumn.

23

Pruning

Other Methods

Annual pruning is rarely necessary for the moderate- or slow-growing shrubs like rhododendrons, heathers and lilacs (syringa), but it pays to remove the spent flower heads carefully to maintain a tidy appearance. You should, however, take great care not to damage the growth buds that lie immediately below the flower trusses and will bear flowers in the following year.

From time to time it may be necessary to cut back severely all types of shrubs to encourage a complete new framework of vigorous young branches. This is often the case where plants have been hit by frost or lain neglected for many years and have in consequence become a tangled mass

of thin and poorly flowered branches; but whenever possible it's best to do the job over several years. Remove about one-third of the old wood completely in the first year, then repeat in subsequent years until the plant is rejuvenated and returned to full vigour.

Where a dense growth of foliage is required, as for instance in the case of hedges and screens, then frequent light prunings may be necessary annually. Privet will need regular clipping throughout the growing season, but coniferous subjects like the Lawson Cypress may be happy with one or two timely cuts. Other evergreens such as holly or laurel usually need only one annual pruning, but for preference use secateurs to do the job rather than shears or power clippers, otherwise the foliage will be badly mutilated and the beauty of the hedge may be marred.

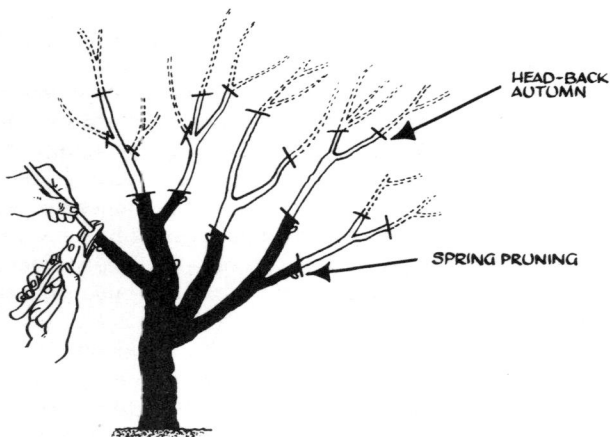

HEAD-BACK AUTUMN

SPRING PRUNING

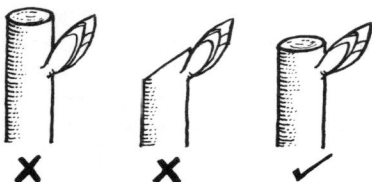

Shrubs that produce flowers on new wood are pruned as shown

Remove dead heads from slow-growing shrubs such as heather or lilac

Neglected plants can be rejuvenated by pruning almost to ground level

A strong pair of secateurs is essential for pruning shrubs. A sharp knife is also very useful for removing odd shoots in awkward positions. Old shrubs may have thick stems that prove too much even for secateurs, so a light pruning saw may be needed to cut them out. A curved-bladed Grecian pruning saw is an ideal tool for the job and you will also find it very useful if there are fruit trees in the garden.

Make sure that all pruning tools are kept sharp to ensure cuts are clean and thus less likely to become infected with fungus diseases, but as a further safeguard treat all large wounds with one of the proprietary wound dressings. Those made of a bitumen base with added fungicide are particularly effective, as they are water repellent and provide an early disease deterrent at the dangerous period when the wound is fresh.

Try to make pruning cuts just above a bud facing in the direction you want a shoot to grow: inwards if the centre of the shrub is bare, but, in the main, growth will be directed outwards to avoid congestion and maintain a good shape. Where you want to retain a naturally weeping habit, branches should be cut back to a convenient downward facing bud to encourage the pendent growth, but for shrubs of an upright or fastigiate form the opposite will be required.

Never leave any snags when pruning, for these frequently die off and provide an ideal breeding ground for pests and diseases. Always cut off large branches flush with the main stem, and cut shoots back to a healthy bud.

Propagation

It's well worth while propagating your own shrubs. Many popular shrubs are easily increased with just a few basic pieces of gardening equipment, and, after a time, when you've gained a little confidence and skill, you'll find yourself attempting the more difficult plants without a second thought.

Shrubs, like other plants, can be increased by sowing seeds, or vegetatively, using cuttings or layering techniques. Raising shrubs from seed can prove a rather long-winded affair, but it is usually the cheapest way to raise a large number of plants where cuttings are not available from your own or a friend's garden. Seeds are sown as normal, into pots or boxes nearly filled with a John Innes or peat seed compost. Large seeds are covered over with about their own depth of compost, while smaller ones are just covered.

Shrubs From Seeds

Good drainage is essential for germination and subsequent healthy growth of seedlings, so if a soil-based compost like John Innes is used, make sure the containers are well crocked with a layer of broken pot or coarse gravel. This is normally unnecessary for peat composts, but a regular check of the drainage slits or holes is wise, to ensure they don't get choked up and cause the compost to waterlog.

Fresh seed will normally germinate far more readily and evenly than old. You can sow shrub seed in the spring in the normal fashion, or as it becomes fully ripened on the tree or shrub. Old or very hard-coated seeds are best sown in the autumn and left in cold frames or under a north-facing wall or fence during the winter.

One little useful trick to 'soften up' hard seeds is to sprinkle them in layers of moist sand in a covered pan or tin during the autumn and stand this in a cold spot outside. The alternate freez-

Cross-section showing seeds planted in a pot

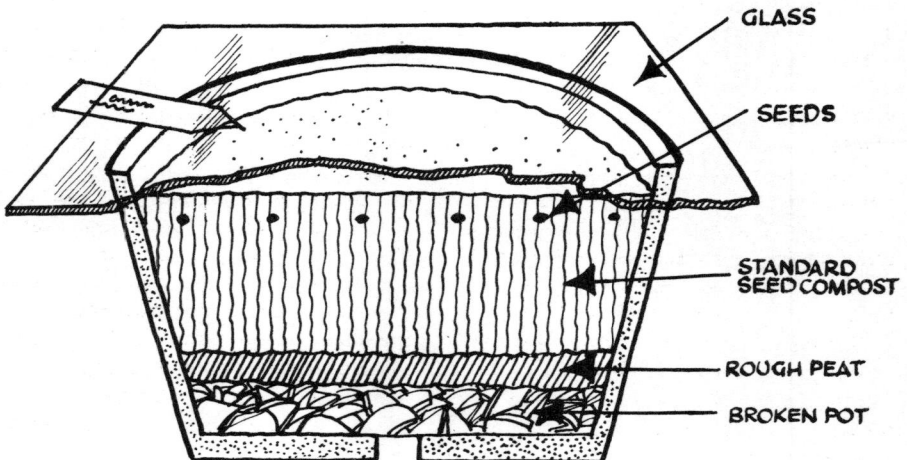

GLASS

SEEDS

STANDARD SEED COMPOST

ROUGH PEAT

BROKEN POT

ing and thawing will help to 'break' the tough outer seed coat and in the spring the seeds can be taken out of the sand and sown in the usual way. This technique is called stratification, and is the amateur's best way of speeding germination of particularly difficult or slow starters.

Where the seeds are large enough to handle individually, the best practice is to space them out over the pot or tray, so that pricking out can be dispensed with and the seedlings can be left undisturbed until large enough to be planted directly into the ground.

Sow fine seeds thinly over the compost surface, cover with sieved compost, gently firm level, then moisten thoroughly using a fine rose on the watering can. Most hardy shrubs will germinate satisfactorily in a cold frame, but if you place the container in a frost-free greenhouse, germination will be that much faster in spring.

Once seedlings have reached a decent size and the tiny leaves can be safely handled without bruising, they can be pricked off into individual small pots filled with fresh, well-drained compost. Take care not to drop the stem of the seedling lower than it was in the original seed container, otherwise it could 'rot off'. Water the plants in, then stand the pots out in a well-ventilated cold frame to grow on to the plantable size.

The most vigorous varieties may require a further move into a larger container in summer, but most will be quite happy in a small pot until planted out in a sheltered 'nursery' plot in the following autumn or spring.

During warm and dry weather, ensure that seedlings do not suffer through want of water, and during the growing season apply a little liquid feed to plants that have filled the pots

with roots. This is especially important if you use one of the peat-based composts, as the plant foods are quickly leached out.

Young seedling shrubs will be more prone to weather damage and pest attack than mature ones, so keep a sharp lookout for signs of distress. If young growth shows the tell-tale 'singeing' around the margins of foliage in early spring, provide some temporary protection from cold, searing winds. Similar symptoms may also occur in summer and this may indicate dehydration through exposure to hot sun or wind.

Use a general insecticide to keep the seedlings clear of common pests such as aphids and caterpillars.

Cuttings

Cuttings offer the best method of propagating shrubs, particularly where a named variety is to be increased. Early in the year when the plants are putting on new growth, soft cuttings can be taken, but it is in the summer period, July to September, that most shrubs provide ideal material. At this time the tips of shoots are still fairly green and flexible, although their bases have ripened and become firm—this is the half-ripe or semi-ripe condition.

Finally, some shrubs are better left until the entire shoot has ripened and entered the hardwood condition. These are prepared and inserted any time from late summer until just before growth starts again in spring.

Soft and half-ripe cuttings usually root fairly rapidly, but hardwood types may take several months before rooting commences, although dipping the cut area of the shoot into a hormone rooting compound may help to speed things up a little.

Propagation

Stem Cuttings

Soft cuttings are taken from the tips of shoots during spring or early summer. Choose vigorous and healthy material and make sure that no pests are present. Cut back the stem just beneath a leaf joint to about 5–10cm (2–4in) long, then trim away any lower surplus leaves—foliage pushed below the surface of the compost will probably rot and could well cause the entire batch of cuttings to die.

Rooting will be quite rapid if you insert the cuttings into pots filled with a sand/peat compost; but to prevent the remaining leaves wilting, place the pots in a propagating frame which should be kept shut down and shaded from bright sun. Alternatively cover the pot with a clean and clear polythene bag until a good root system has formed in the compost.

Half-ripe cuttings taken later in the year can be similarly treated, but they are usually left a little longer and the base of the trimmed stem should be of firm current year's wood. Where only short sideshoots are available, trimming may be impracticable, so the best method is to pull them away complete with a 'heel' of older wood. As the rooting end of the half-ripe cuttings is rather firm, dipping them into rooting compound will often be advantageous, although not absolutely essential.

Insert the cuttings into pots or directly into the soil base of frames where peat and sand have been worked in. It's important not to allow them to dry out or be scorched by hot sun. Half-ripe cuttings struck in summer can be overwintered in cold frames and planted out the following year.

Hardwood cuttings taken late in the year, when in fact top growth is slowing down or has stopped, will take some time to root. These are normally inserted either in a sandy frame bed or outside in a sheltered position where the ground is well drained. Roses, forsythia and a range of hedging shrubs including privet and hawthorn are quite readily raised in this fashion.

Sturdy shoots about the thickness of a pencil are suitable, trimming the bases to below a leaf joint, or to a bud in the case of the deciduous types that have dropped their foliage. Depending on the material, cuttings should be about 20.5–25.5cm (8–10in) in length, half of which will be inserted into the soil. Hormone rooting powder is a distinct advantage with this type of cutting, for the well-ripened wood is by nature slow to callus and form roots.

In the open, all you need to do is to make a V-shaped cleft in the ground with a spade, then line the base with a generous helping of sharp sand. Push the prepared shoots down into this, then firm back the soil with your foot. Hardwood cuttings will be well-rooted enough to be moved into their final quarters in one or two years' time.

Leaf-bud Cuttings

Apart from straightforward stem cuttings, there are one or two other methods employed for certain shrubs. Camellias can also be propagated by leaf-bud cuttings, a sharp razor blade or knife being used to slice out a portion of ripe stem containing a healthy leaf complete with the small dormant bud—don't choose the tempting fat ones, for these are the flower buds. These can then be dibbled in to a lime-free moist compost and placed in a polythene bag or closed frame where they won't dry out.

Preparing half-ripe cuttings

Propagation

Internodal Cuttings

The long stems of climbers like clematis can be cut into sections giving a number of plants from just one shoot. Choose half-ripened wood of the current year and cut it into sections, each bearing one pair of leaves and buds. Whereas most stem cuttings are trimmed back to just below a leaf joint and termed 'nodal cuttings', clematis are treated slightly differently. Here the sections of stem are prepared so that about 2.5–5cm (1–2in) of the stem remains below the leaves and they are trimmed off cleanly just above the pair of buds. After dipping the stems in a rooting compound, insert so that the leaf joint is just about touching the compost.

Layering

In cases where shrubs are known to be very slow-rooting, eg magnolias, evergreen rhododendrons and some climbers, layering may provide an answer. Where shoots can be pulled down to ground level, they can be partially severed on the underside with a sharp knife, then pegged down into soil improved by the addition of some peat and sharp sand. It's important that ground layers are firmly fixed below the soil and kept moist at all times, otherwise rooting will not take place.

Apart from the difficult subjects, this method is also very good for propagating numbers of popular plants like winter jasmine and old heathers that have become straggly and bare towards the base of the stems.

In some cases, the shrub may not have branches supple or low enough to be pegged down to the ground, but here you could try aerial layering (which, incidentally, can also be used to tidy up a straggling specimen of the popular Indian rubber plant indoors).

The technique is to make a sloping cut up into the stem just beneath a leaf joint—but no more than halfway through or it may snap off prematurely. Place a small wad of damp moss into the wound after working some rooting powder into the cut, then bind the whole area with a generous wrapping of moistened sphagnum moss (available from florists). Finally cover the whole wad with black polythene and tape up thoroughly to prevent drying out. If you have difficulty getting moss, you could use coarse peat as a substitute, but make sure it's moss peat and not the sedge type.

Layers prepared in late summer or autumn often show signs of rooting by the following spring, but the very hard-wooded plants like the shrubby magnolias (*M. stellata*) and rhododendrons may need a little more time before the shoots can be completely severed and lifted. The great advantage of layering, however, is that provided you don't cut into the stems too deeply, even if they fail to root on the first attempt you can try again.

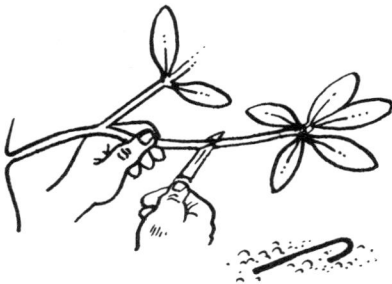

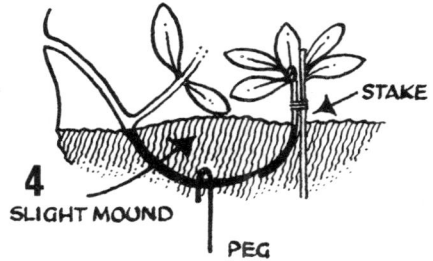

Method of layering shrubs:
1. prepare the soil beneath the shoot
2. remove the lower leaves
3. partially cut the stem
4. peg the stem firmly into the soil

Shrub Troubles

Many shrubs are remarkably free of troubles, but from time to time poor growth and discoloured foliage may indicate that something is wrong. From the start it pays to watch out for tell-tale signs of attack by pest or disease —when you first select your plants at the nursery or garden centre, then periodically throughout each successive season of growth.

Good cultivation will of course lessen the effects of pest and disease, for plants, like ourselves, will put up more resistance if in a vigorous condition. Hygiene is most important, so don't allow heaps of rubbish or leaves to accumulate in or under shrubs for any length of time—these are always ideal hiding places for pests and a breeding ground for numerous fungal disorders, like honey fungus.

Damaged or dead branches can also be a starting point for disease, so these should be repaired or removed promptly. A regular spraying programme starting early in the year will also minimize troubles. Small populations of pests are far easier to control early on than if you ignore the trouble and have to face an explosion of 'bugs' in the warm conditions of spring and summer.

Deciduous shrubs will benefit from being treated with a winter tar oil wash in January or early February, but take care that any 'green' plants nearby or underneath are covered with a protective sheet of newspaper or polythene. Such treatment early in the year should kill off many sucking insect eggs laid in the previous year, and so give you a reasonably clean start to the season. Continue spraying from spring onwards, however, using one of the broad spectrum pesticides to forestall any survivors or fresh arrivals from building up new colonies.

If you do have to use chemical sprays, choose a dull, windless day so that spray drift is minimized and there's little chance of foliage being 'scorched' by sun. Also remember to avoid spraying plants that are in flower, for apart from possible discoloration of blooms occurring, you will also put at risk visiting beneficial insects such as bees.

Deep-set fungus diseases like coral spot or the bracket fungi, that often start off on dead wood and move into live tissue later, should be cut out completely. Spraying will have no effect on these, as the 'roots' (mycelium) are usually well down in the wood. But fungicides, such as those based on benomyl, may have the desired effect on 'surface' diseases that attack foliage and soft new stems.

The wide variety of powdery mildew diseases and black spot on roses can be controlled by using benomyl or other systemic fungicides as the symptoms are noticed, but it pays to carry on the treatment at regular intervals to prevent re-infection.

Infected prunings and fallen leaves are best collected up and burnt for safety. Never use such material for composting, as this will only spread the trouble later when the compost is used for mulching or digging in.

Apart from pest and disease troubles, occasionally a shrub may show signs of distress without any visible outward cause. In such cases the problem may lie at soil level, through an imbalance of plant foods or incorrect drainage. Certain shrubs have a special 'taste' for a particular soil type, the ericaceous group being typical, as these prefer an acid soil and resent

(above) spraying shrub with pesticide; (below) where shrub stems are fixed to a wall, swellings may develop around the ties

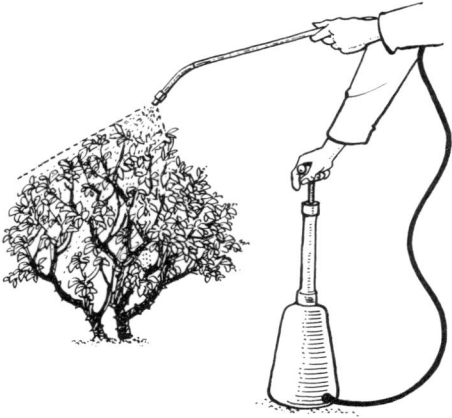

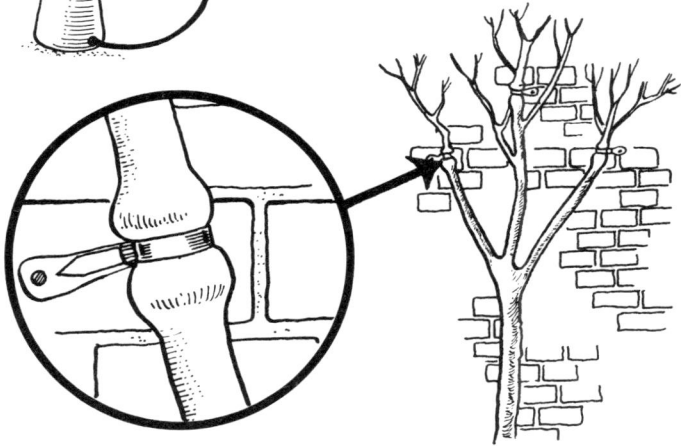

lime in any form. Symptoms of excess lime usually show in paling foliage and white streaking. If the trouble is very local, as in the case of artificial liming in a previous season, then application of sequestered iron should help— otherwise the best bet is to grow only lime-tolerant shrubs.

Other symptoms of plant-food imbalance in the soil may occur, such as stunted highly coloured growth, but these are relatively rare on most decent garden soils. Wilting and general shrub decline, however, may be a sign that drainage is either too severe or impaired to such an extent that the roots are waterlogged.

In both cases the fault was probably initiated at the planting stage, which emphasizes how important site or planting-hole preparation is. In such cases, provided the shrub is small enough to lift in autumn, the best policy is to start from scratch and do a thorough job.

Constriction is also liable to weaken stems and cause the branches to snap in high winds. This is a common trouble with climbing shrubs tied to walls and shows clearly with the stems of woody types swelling around the ties. To avoid damage of this sort, periodically check the ties and loosen any that appear tight round the shoots.

Shrub Types

Climbing Shrubs

Many of our most beautiful garden plants fall under this heading. They are equally useful at giving interest at high and low levels; given the freedom of rambling over a shed or useless tree they make superb camouflage, whereas if they are carefully trained and tied in to support wires running along a low wall or fence, a blanketing effect can be obtained, as with a hedge.

Support in some form or other is essential if climbing shrubs are to look their best. If you do not have a convenient old tree stump, rustic poles can be set into the ground, either singly or linked to form a pergola, and the shoots trained up these by tying into strong galvanized or plastic covered wires. Wires should be secured firmly by attaching them to rawl bolts, rings or wall nails set into brickwork, or stapled into wooden supports at regular intervals.

On walls and fences, climbers with masses of thin shoots are more easily dealt with by training them up trellises made of wooden lathes, or by using one of the many proprietary plastic-covered trellises. The plastic mesh netting now available for climbers is also very useful and can be bought in various colours to suit the situation.

Where wooden supports are employed, it's essential that these are given thorough preservative treatment to prevent rotting. But take care that plants do not make contact with wood treated with creosote unless you can be absolutely sure that all the harmful fumes have disappeared. Remember that it will be very difficult to remove climbers from trellises after they have become established, so make sure that the preservative treatment is a good one.

Where wall nails or staples need to be used, these should be galvanized to prevent rusting. Iron nails will soon rust away in the open and this may allow the shrubs to fall away from a wall. Where large climbers are planted, the nails or raw bolts must be large enough to support the weight, especially during windy weather; this also applies to the thickness (gauge) of wires used for training.

Although self-clinging shrubs such as ivies and those producing 'sucker pads' on the shoots, can be safely

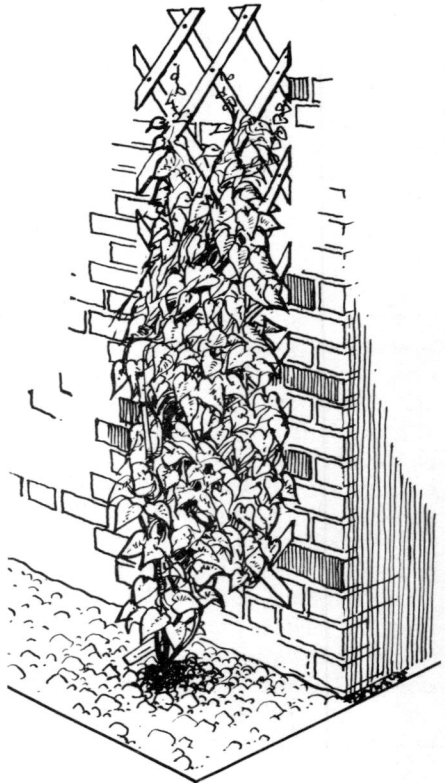

allowed to grow directly against modern brickwork, it is best to keep them away from old buildings where lime mortar was used. But where any climber is trained up a dwelling house, remember that you will need to carry out maintenance and repairs from time to time, so make sure that windows, guttering and similar areas are kept free from dense vegetation.

Growing on a trellis is the best answer here, for then the whole support can be let down complete with the shrub, so that you can get to the area needing attention without resorting to hacking the plant about.

Many of the less dense deciduous climbers can be used to brighten up a drab conifer or sizeable fruit tree, but it is a mistake to plant rampant types, like Russian vine, on living trees. The ultimate effect may be quite eye-catching during the summer period, but in winter when both climber and 'host' are bare of leaves, you may find the tree gradually dying through lack of light.

Pick of the Climbers

Actinidia kolomikta
This beautiful foliage plant can reach up to 6m (20ft) high, but can be horizontally trained to give low-level colour. The leaves are green with white and pink markings.

Ampelopsis brevipedunculata
An ornametal vine with hop-like foliage which grips by means of tendrils. Blue berries are produced after warm summer weather. Ideal for covering large areas of bleak walls, sheds or drab hedges.

Campsis 'Madame Galen'
An exotic flowering climber producing clusters of beautiful red trumpets, provided it's in good light. Needs support from an early age and is good for trailing over walls or fences.

Celastrus orbiculatus
One of the most attractive twining shrubs for covering an unsightly feature such as a dead tree stump. Thin wiry growths are covered with fruits which split to reveal bright yellow interiors, setting off the red seeds to perfection. The leaves turn bright yellow before dropping in autumn. Where only one celastrus is planted, choose the hermaphrodite form with flowers of both sexes present, otherwise berries may not form.

Hedera colchica 'Dentata Variegata'
Probably the best rampant variegated ivy offered, with the largest leaves of the entire genus. A superb all-year evergreen for covering walls, fences or any other unsightly garden feature. Roots grow from the stems, so avoid planting against old brickwork laid with lime mortar. This Persian ivy will grow in almost any soil or situation.

Hydrangea petiolaris
The climbing hydrangea. Ideal for clothing a north-facing wall or any other shaded position. Self-clinging stems are clothed with toothed, pointed foliage and the heads of white flowers are produced during June. Also good for camouflaging old tree stumps.

Shrub Types

Pick of the Climbers
Jasminum nudiflorum
Although not strictly a climber, the evergreen arching stems of this species can be trained and tied in to wires to provide wall cover up to reasonable heights. The flowers are produced from

Jasminum nudiflorum

early winter through to spring and are deep yellow in colour. The summer jasmine, *J. officinale,* forms a substantial trunk when established, from which sprout slender shoots bearing sweetly scented clusters of white, trumpet-like flowers. They prefer a sunny position, but the summer jasmine needs a protected spot in cold, exposed districts.

Lonicera japonica 'Aureoreticulata'
This foliage honeysuckle has small, bright green leaves with yellow venation. Evergreen, vigorous and easy, it makes an ideal screening plant on net fencing or trailing over a wall. For flowering qualities, try 'Belgica', the early Dutch honeysuckle, with reddish-purple flower clusters fading to yellow and sweetly scented.

Polygonum baldschuanicum
The notorious Russian vine, or more aptly the mile-a-minute vine. This is a particularly rampant climber which can soon cover walls, sheds or nearby trees, so be careful where you site it. As it suckers prodigiously from the base, cutting it back severely will encourage even stronger growth. Kept within the confines of a small bed running along a wall, or trained over a dead tree, it can be very effective, with trailing growths literally smothered with pink-tinged white flower clusters throughout summer.

Solanum crispum
A semi-evergreen shrub with large clusters of violet potato-like flowers in late summer. A good plant for chalk soils, but site it in a sheltered south- or south-west-facing position to get best results. It can be trained against a wall or trailed over fences and small sheds.

Wisteria sinensis
The Chinese wisteria can reach up to 30m (100ft) when mature, but is normally found much lower, trained on a wall or over pergolas. The drooping clusters of mauve or lilac flowers resemble laburnum and are produced in late spring, although some plants may take several years before showing signs of flowering. A full-sun position is best, as this will encourage the wood to ripen and produce buds.

Wisteria sinensis

Clematis

This is probably the most popular of all climbing shrubs, for it is both relatively easy to grow and produces prolific amounts of bloom during spring and summer, followed by attractive fluffy seed heads. It climbs by winding its leaf stalks around anything within range, and some of the more vigorous species are superb for covering vast areas with colour. The large-flowered hybrids are not generally so vigorous, but make superb plants for training on trellises.

Clematis like a moist cool root run and do best when the lower area of the stems are within the shade of other plants. Where the root area is exposed to sun, placing tiles on the ground will help keep the soil cool and moist during the summer months.

Many people are confused when it comes to pruning clematis, but if you know what the plant is, then the job should be fairly straightforward. Generally, species like *C. montana* and its varieties, *C. orientalis*, *C. macropetala* and *C. florida*, need only light pruning to keep them within bounds. Remove dead shoots and shorten any growths that are getting out of the space allocated to them on trellises. Where late-flowering species need to be kept fairly low, say on a fence, then they can be cut back to about 30cm (12in) from the ground early in spring, otherwise they tend to get leggy and rather bare at the base.

The large flowered hybrids are similarly pruned, restricting hard pruning to the later flowering varieties such as 'Jackmanii', 'Ville de Lyon' and 'Lady Betty Balfour'. The earlier varieties flowering in May and June are pruned lightly after flowering, removing dead or weak growth and shortening flowered lateral shoots back slightly to keep them tidy and encourage a second flush of bloom later in the year. Varieties treated in this fashion include 'Nelly Moser', 'The President', 'Vyvian Pennell', 'Lasurstern' and 'Barbara Dibley'.

Species

C. alpina: ideal scrambling species for low walls, low shrubs or the rock garden. The solitary flowers are blue and produced in spring.

C. armandii: a vigorous evergreen climber with groups of three large, leathery dark green leaves and clusters of creamy white flowers in spring. As the growth can be damaged by severe weather, give it a sheltered, sunny position.

C. florida: the flowers of this delicate species recall those of the passion flower. The outer sepals are white with a green stripe and the central boss of petaloid stamens is violet. Flowers in early summer.

Shrub Types

Clematis

C. macropetala: in good conditions this species will cover a wall with its unusual double sky-blue blooms from May onwards. The variety 'Markham's Pink' is of a pale pink shade. Also of interest for the silky seed heads that follow flowering.

Clematis macropetala

C. montana: one of the most popular and easy species of early spring-flowering types. Medium-sized flowers are produced abundantly and according to variety; colours include creamy-white, pink and rose. Ideal for covering up unsightly features such as a concrete garage, large unproductive fruit trees and bleak walls. Good varieties include, 'Elizabeth' (soft pink), rubens (bronze-purple shoots, pink flowers) and grandiflora (white).

C. tangutica: another rampant grower, but with rather small leaves. The flowers are very prolific and resemble deep yellow lanterns. The petals are very thick and reminiscent of orange peel, which gives rise to its common name 'orange-peel clematis'. *C. orientalis* is similar, but not considered quite as good in the yellow-flowered group. Summer flowering.

Hybrids

Ernest Markham: rounded petals of a beautiful petunia-red, with an attractive sheen. Flowers June to September.

Gravetye Beauty: unusual bell-shaped flowers of cherry-red, which gradually open out with age. Flowers from July to September.

Jackmanii Superba: Large rich purple-violet blooms during late summer. One of the most vigorous hybrids grown today and superb for trellises and arbors.

Lasurstern: tapering, wavy-edged blooms in lavender-blue in late spring and early summer. The flowers are large and set off by the central white cluster of stamens.

Nelly Moser: probably the best-known large-flowered clematis today. Free flowering, but best when grown against a north-facing wall to prevent the flowers getting bleached by sun. Petals are mauve-pink with a central bar of carmine. Flowers in May and June, and often produces a second flush later in the year.

Ville de Lyon: bright carmine-red blooms with contrasting golden stamens. A good one for a late show in early autumn.

Vyvian Pennell: a double variety with violet-blue blooms suffused with carmine-purple towards the central region of the flower. Fully double-flowers from May to July, but some single lavender blooms may be produced later in the season.

Shrubs for Foliage and Stem Colour

Although colourful flowers may be the prime requirement of many people, we should not forget the value of shrubs that produce bold and colourful foliage. These often provide a longer period of interest than the flowers themselves and during the summer months act as a coloured backcloth to blooms, whilst in the winter period they prevent a rather bare and bleak appearance if evergreens are liberally dotted here and there.

The bark and twigs of certain shrubs may also brighten up the winter scene, particularly if smaller types are grouped together to form a special feature, with a backing of conifers or other evergreens to act as a foil.

Aucuba japonica (Japanese Laurel)

For dark and overcast positions, this is the shrub to choose. It will put up with dry, poorish soils, although given a decent fertile site and good light, selected named forms will give a good account of themselves. 'Crotonifolia' has bold evergreen leaves blotched

Aucuba japonica

and spotted with gold, whilst 'Variegata' shows prominent speckling in gold.

The individual varieties are available in single sexes only, so if you want berries, choose a male form like 'Crotonifolia' to pollinate female plants such as 'Variegata'. Pruning is required only if the odd branch turns brown after severe drought, or when the strong stems begin to get congested—prune the latter down to the ground in spring.

Berberis thunbergii 'Atropurpurea Nana'

This shrub will grow anywhere, provided the ground is not waterlogged. This is a dwarf form which can be safely planted where room is at a premium, and makes an ideal attractive low hedge or rock-garden shrub. The leaves are purple-red and the flowers are small and yellow. *B. thunbergii* 'Atropurpurea' also bears the coloured foliage, but is much taller and more suitable for a large shrub border.

Light pruning will be necessary only from time to time. Just cut away any dead stems.

Calluna vulgaris 'Aurea'

This variety of golden heather has purple flowers from August until September. The foliage is gold-tinted during the growing season, but takes on a bronzey hue in autumn. Like all heathers, it dislikes lime in the soil, preferring acid conditions, but the addition of peat to the ground will keep it happy.

Like all heaths, pruning is restricted to trimming over the plants in spring to remove dead flower heads so the new growth can develop unimpeded. Besides this particular variety, there are numerous other coloured foliage forms available with various flower colours.

Shrub Types

Shrubs for Foliage and Stem Colour

Philadelphus coronarius 'Aureus'

This golden-leaved form of Mock Orange is medium sized and most attractive when in flower. The young leaves are bright yellow, turning yellowish green as they mature. The flowers are white and scented.

Thin out weak growths and old flowered stems that are becoming unproductive immediately after blooms fade in summer. Cut back to within 2.5cm (1in) of the ground or main stem.

Rubus cockburnianus

This ornamental bramble is well worth searching out for the medium-sized arching branches it produces, bearing fern-like foliage. The stems are purple, but this is almost obscured by the layer of silvery white 'bloom' covering them. The undersides of the foliage are similarly covered. The fruits and flowers are insignificant.

To maintain a succession of beautiful canes, cut the stems right down annually immediately after flowering— exactly as you would treat raspberry plants.

Elaeagnus pungens 'Maculata'

A moderate growing 'evergreen' shrub with striking mid-green foliage, handsomely marked with a central splash of bright gold-yellow. This shrub will grow on almost any soil, except on very shallow soils overlaying solid chalk. The undersides of the foliage are covered with a rusty brown 'felt' and the plant is very resistant to wind and salty conditions near the coast.

Little pruning will be needed, but cut out any shoots that bear green

Elaeagnus pungens 'Maculata'

leaves only, otherwise the whole shrub may quickly revert to the unmarked type species.

Rosa omiensis pteracantha

A densely growing rose species which produces distinctive stems covered with broad and flattened crimson spines. It is not suitable for planting where children can reach it easily, but is good for discouraging unwanted pets in the garden. The flowers are small, usually white, and followed by pear-shaped crimson and yellow fruits.

Prune back flowered stems annually or biennially to encourage strong new growth from the base of the plant.

Cornus alba 'Spaethii'

This is the golden variegated-leaved form of the red-barked dogwood. Each plant makes a thicket of dark red stems which give a colourful splash during the winter months when the leaves have dropped. During the spring and summer, the plants are clothed with most attractive green and gold foliage.

To keep the plant from getting straggly, cut back the shoots hard almost to ground level in spring, just as the buds begin to break out. This is done every second year. The yellow-stemmed *C. stolonifera* 'Flaviramea' makes a good companion plant, particularly if groups of both varieties can be planted—they are ideal for damp or boggy soils near water.

Cotinus coggygria

Cotinus coggygria 'Royal Purple'
Popularly called the smoke tree, this is a strong-growing shrub reaching up to about 3.6m (12ft) in the strongest forms. 'Royal Purple' is a very dramatic form with wine-purple rounded leaves and plume-like flower heads in early summer. The colour of the foliage reddens towards autumn.

If no regular pruning is done, cotinus forms a strong-growing bush, but if a framework of main branches is first developed, shoots can be cut hard back each spring to leave two strong buds. In this way the shrub can be kept under strict control in a restricted space, but no flowers will be produced.

Weigelia florida 'Variegata'
This forms a compact, medium-sized shrub which in the growing season is clothed with creamy edged green foliage. It is one of the most popular variegated shrubs grown today, for in addition to the foliage effect, this particular variety produces numerous pink flowers during late spring and early summer. Occasionally a second flush of bloom is produced during late summer or autumn.

As the flowers are produced on growth made in the previous year, cut back flowered shoots to the main branches after blooms have faded.

Shrub Types

Shrubs for Fruit Display

In many cases, shrubs provide a bonus display of richly coloured fruits after flowering. With several, the berry harvest surpasses the flower display in beauty, although birds may take a percentage of the crop for food—an asset if you are interested in attracting a wide variety of wild life into your garden.

When planning out the positions of your shrubs, it's a good idea to site the berrying shrubs evenly throughout, to spread the area of interest during the autumn and winter months. Try to situate them where the crop of bright fruits will not be obscured by evergreens and away from paths where the fallen fruit could be trodden on and taken indoors on your shoes.

Callicarpa bodinieri

A neat medium-sized shrub producing long foliage which turns rose-purple in the autumn before falling, plus a crop of attractive lilac fruits after flowering. As callicarpa is not good at self-pollinating, group two or three plants together to ensure a good crop of berries.

Cotoneaster 'Hybridus Pendulus'

A fairly low-growing evergreen shrub, which can also be obtained trained as a weeping standard. The foliage is long and glossy and held on prostrate branches, which bear whitish clusters of flowers followed by bright red berries during the autumn and winter months. The standard form is ideal for using as a specimen shrub in a small bed cut out of a lawn and the low-growing normal form can be used to advantage for ground cover effect.

Pernettya mucronata

Pernettya mucronata

This is a lime hater that revels in light peaty soils. It forms dense evergreen clumps of 0.9m (3ft) stems which bear numerous small white flowers followed by berries in white, pink or red. Plant in groups for good berry set, including one good male form such as 'Edward Balls'. Pernettyas are happy in full sun or half shade conditions.

Passiflora caerulea

This is the common passion flower, a climbing shrub needing a sheltered south- or south-west-facing wall or fence to succeed. It needs good drainage, but avoid deep rich soils which tend to encourage rampant growth at the expense of flowers and fruit. The flowers are large and most exotic in appearance, with white outer parts and a central arrangement of blue and white filaments. The large egg-shaped fruits are orange-red and produced more abundantly during very warm summers. In mild districts the common passion flower is evergreen. Quite severe thinning of shoots may be required in spring to avoid congestion, and new growths should be tied in to wires set horizontally along the wall or fence.

Pyracantha 'Watereri'

This hybrid firethorn has a compact growth habit and can be trained against a wall or carefully pruned to form an impenetrable hedge. The white flower clusters are produced in summer and followed by beautiful red fruits, which in good years can almost mask the foliage. A sunny position is required if the wood is to ripen sufficiently to initiate good annual flower and fruit production.

Rosa moyesii

Rosa moyesii 'Geranium'

This is a compact form of the species, bearing geranium-coloured single blooms about 7.5cm (3in) across. The flagon-shaped fruits are dark red and quite large and grouped on short shoots protruding from branches. It is a medium-sized rose with an upright, open habit—the flowering period is June and July.

Skimmia japonica

This small evergreen shrub is ideal for all types of soils and situations. As plants bear either male or female flowers only, it's necessary to plant them in pairs or groups of one male to several female forms. 'Foremanii' is a good berry-producing female form with broad leaves and large clusters of red fruit which persist throughout winter. 'Fragrans' would make an ideal partner, as the flowers are sweetly scented and male.

Symphoricarpus orbiculatus

Better known as the coral berry, this easy shrub is ideal for dark positions under tall shrubs or trees and does fairly well even in dry soil conditions. The fruits are deep-rose-coloured and similar to the familiar common snowberry which is frequently seen planted in park shrubberies. It makes a dense growth habit up to about 2m (6ft).

Viburnum davidii

A less-well-known species which is desirable for its low growth habit and evergreen foliage, as well as for the unusual turquoise-blue berries. As individual plants may be all-male or all-female, group planting is advisable, although containerized plants bearing berries should prove trustworthy. This attractive shrub is ideal for small gardens or large rock gardens and forms a distinctive mound shape when established.

Viburnum opulus

This shrub is best known as the guelder rose and produces maple-like leaves on vigorous bushes. The white flowers are reminiscent of lacecap hydrangeas and produced in summer. These are followed by large bunches of bright red fruits which last well into winter. The variety 'Compactum' is perhaps better for smaller gardens and 'Notcutt's Variety' has larger flowers and fruits than the native wild type. 'Xanthocarpum' has beautiful yellow fruits; all have good autumn leaf colour.

Flowering Shrubs for Every Month

Even in a modest-sized garden, there's no reason why you shouldn't enjoy shrub flowers in every month of the year. The following have been chosen for their good nature and all will give a brave show provided the soil is well drained and moderately fertile.

They can be grouped together to form a calendar of colour, or dotted about the garden in positions chosen to set each off to the best advantage. You probably won't want to trek down the garden during the colder months, so late-flowering types are better planted near the house where they can be seen in comfort.

January

Viburnum bodnantense

This medium-to-large hybrid shrub displays a strong upright habit, making it a good choice for a back position in the border. The bare branches produce clusters of densely packed flowers of deep pink any time from October onwards, but the best displays are usually during January and February.

The blooms are very sweetly scented and appear to disregard frosts totally, so it can be planted in a fairly open situation quite safely. There are several named forms available, 'Dawn' probably being the most popular.

As this shrub has a pronounced stooling habit, with shoots growing freely from the base, pruning can be restricted to removing a few very old stems near to ground level as the young growths threaten to congest the bush. Prune after flowering until winter.

February

Mahonia japonica

A beautiful evergreen shrub with tall erect stems bearing dark green pinnate leaves reminiscent of holly, but much more attractive. The flowers are small, but densely clustered on long lax spikes which spill out from the tips of shoots during the winter months. As a bonus, the lemon-yellow blooms are fragrant.

Mahonia japonica

Little or no pruning is required, although dead wood should be removed. Cutting back to a bud near ground level, into live tissue, should encourage replacement stems.

All hardy mahonias thrive in any decent garden soil, including chalky ones, provided the site is well drained.

March

Daphne mezereum

A sweetly scented shrub ideal for very chalky soils, although it will grow in most types of ground. The purplish-red flowers are borne on short stalks up the stem on wood made in the previous year. There is also an attractive white form offered, which like the red type produces poisonous berries after flowering.

This shrub never reaches large proportions, and so is ideal for the small garden and front positions in the border. Daphne bushes are best left undisturbed and pruning should be restricted to removing dead wood only.

April

Forsythia 'Lynwood'

Probably the most spectacular variety available of this easy and popular plant; it reaches quite modest heights in a very short time. The strong shoots are smothered in large, deep-yellow blooms.

Forsythia Lynwood

Pruning should be done immediately after flowering, taking out weak, thin growths that produced little or no flowers, and a proportion of very tough older flowered wood. The latter should be cut down almost to the ground or to a convenient strong lateral shoot.

May

Kerria japonica

A tall-growing shrub with a suckering growth habit. Very easy to grow, but it should be thinned out periodically immediately after flowering to prevent the bush becoming congested and unsightly. The green arching stems are covered with bright yellow, buttercup-like flowers for quite long periods in spring. The double form 'Pleniflora' is slightly more attractive in flower and is often listed under the name 'Flore Pleno'.

Use secateurs to prune old flowered stems down to the ground, and thin out excess weak growth to allow strong stems to develop unimpeded.

June

Deutzia elegantissima

This produces rather loose heads of rose-pink, scented flowers that open from the outside of the cluster first. They need a sunny spot to prevent the bush from becoming straggly and flowering poorly.

Cut back flowered shoots to within 2.5cm (1in) of older wood to promote new growth which will bear blooms in the following year. As this shrub makes a lot of new growth from below ground, also remove a proportion of large old stems completely to maintain a symmetrical, fairly open habit. Grows about 2m (6ft) high.

Flowering Shrubs for Every Month

July

Buddleia davidii
Perhaps better known as the Butterfly Bush, this shrub is a rapid grower and ideal as a filler while more long-lived shrubs are getting established. Many varieties are offered by nurserymen, but take care to pick reliable named sorts which will give good colours—many of the unnamed plants offered come in very washy, pale shades!

Good varieties include 'Black Knight', a rich deep violet, 'Fascination', with large spikes of lilac-pink, and 'Peace', a scented white type.

This shrub will soon get very tall and unshapely if not pruned back hard annually before flowering. Build up a strong framework of permanent branches on a sturdy stem about 30.5cm (1ft) high and hard-prune these back each year as you would bush roses.

August

Fuchsia 'Mrs Popple'
Vigorous growing, particularly in the south and coastal areas. Small habit but bearing large flowers with scarlet upper sepals and violet petals; the protruding stamens and style are crimson. In colder districts protection may be necessary, for fuchsias can be cut back to ground level by severe frost. Cover stems with bracken in autumn to minimize damage as much as possible.

In spring, cut out all dead growth and shorten stems killed by frost back to a point where new shooots are breaking out vigorously. After severe winters it is often necessary to cut the stems right down to encourage a flush of strong new replacement shoots from the base.

September

Hebe 'Midsummer Beauty'
This is a moderately hardy hybrid of small dimensions, which is best in a sheltered but well-lit position to produce an abundance of the long lavender flower spikes during summer. The leaves are conspicuously coloured red on the undersides.

Hebes are often incorrectly listed as veronicas, the latter name being now restricted to their herbaceous cousins only. As they are liable to get badly cut back by frost, some hard pruning may be necessary in spring, using the new shoots as a guide to making cuts. Cut back each branch to a strong shoot, taking care to leave an evenly shaped bush once the job is completed.

Hibiscus syriacus

October

Hibiscus syriacus

Normally hibiscus are associated with tropical islands, but this species is perfectly at home in our changeable climate. Many varieties are offered, both single and double flowered, ranging in colour from pure white like 'Snowdrift', through lilac and mauve shades to the violet-blue 'Blue Bird'. In good conditions it can reach small tree-like proportions, but normally bushes reach about 1.8m (6ft) or so high.

Little pruning is necessary, apart from removing any dead or damaged branches in spring or summer. Occasionally some harder pruning may be necessary on established specimens to thin out overgrown growth—do this in spring, removing even amounts of wood throughout the shrub.

November

Erica carnea

Varieties of this lovely Alpine species of heath are numerous, white, pink and red flowers being available. They make dense hummocky growth and flower for long periods throughout the winter period. This is one heath that will tolerate some lime in the soil, although it will not succeed on shallow and very chalky ground. 'Eileen Porter' is a rich red variety which can be had in flower from October until April.

Although heaths will grow in light shade, best growth and depth of flower colour is obtained when they are grouped in an open position. In most years pruning can be reduced to clipping over the plants to remove dead flower heads as they turn brown—this will encourage new shoots to grow away and keep the plants nice and compact. Hard pruning is necessary only when older plants begin to look straggly.

December

Hamamelis mollis

Perhaps better known as the Chinese Witch Hazel, this large shrub has unusual papery flowers in shades of yellow, the largest of which are produced by the variety 'Pallida'. The flowers appear on bare branches from December onwards and are sweetly scented; on grafted plants blooms are quite prolific even at an early age. The foliage too is decorative, giving good yellow autumn colour before the leaves finally fall.

Provided hamamelis is planted in good light, it is best left to take on its natural shape and little or no pruning is necessary. If pruning is needed, do it after the flowers have faded, but before growth commences in spring.

Illustrated by Barry Gurbutt

British Library Cataloguing in Publication Data

Edwards, Ray
    Choosing and caring for garden shrubs.
    —(Penny pinchers).
    1. Shrubs
    I. Title II. Series
    635.9'76   SB435

    ISBN 0–7153–7902–X

Text and illustrations
© David & Charles Ltd 1980

Printed in Great Britain
by A. Wheaton & Co., Ltd., Exeter
for David & Charles (Publishers) Limited
Brunel House   Newton Abbot   Devon